Egghead the Movie

Written by Michael Lacey Freeman

Illustrated by Bethany Lacey-Freeman & Craig Bulloch

EGGHEAD THE MOVIE

Independently Published by:
Michael Lacey Freeman, Italy
Email: michaellaceyfreeman@gmail.com
www.michaellaceyfreeman.com
© All rights reserved.

Published 2023
ISBN: 978-1-7394459-0-4

_____

BONUS STORY
Mr Smart
By Michael Lacey Freeman

Michael Lacey Freeman

egghead
the movie

Illustrated by
Bethany Lacey-Freeman
Craig Bulloch

*"I'm the best, I'm the worst
I'm the last, I'm the first
I'm in chains, I am free
I am you, you are me
Can you hear me?*

I'm telling my story"

(from the song, 'Crying' 2017, Paoloni & Lacey Freeman)

Contents

Chapter 1: Strawberry Day

Monday January 23rd, 2017

Hi! My name's Emily28!
That's my name on Twitter and Instagram and everywhere else I go on the Internet. But it's not my real
name.
My real name is . . .
Well, I'll tell you later. For now, it's a secret. For now,
my name is Emily28. You can't see me, and I can't
see you, and it's better that way. No one at school
uses my real name anyway. They call me something
else.
Everyone in my class calls me . . .

Farm Girl

And they call me this because I'm the new girl. I
come from another place called Norwich. They think
that it's a boring place in the countryside where
nothing happens.   A place that only your nan or
grandad visits. But they only think that because they
don't know it.
Norwich is beautiful and they should see it for them-
selves before they say these things.

Now I go to a new school, in a new place, but I
haven't got any new friends.

'You'll be fine,' says my mum.
'You'll soon make new friends,' says my dad.
But it's not easy.
The other children at my new school don't like me.
It's as simple as that. I'm different from them.

I think a lot about my old life in Norwich. What do I miss?

1. Walking out of my house on 28a Cardiff Road and knowing everyone and everything I see.

2. Sitting by the river and drawing. I love drawing and I do it all the time. When I have a problem, I draw, and it helps me to feel better. I'm drawing something special now. I'll never show it to anyone. Not even you.

3. Sitting on the steps with friends outside a place called, the Forum and watching YouTube videos and going for a pizza on Magdalen Street.

4. Spending time with Isabella and chatting about anything and everything. I miss Isabella most of all. Isabella is my best friend. I can't see her because she still lives in Norwich. But we chat almost every day.

My pets are my friends too! They'll always be happy to see me. Bob is my dog and Mango is my cat. When I come home, Bob is always happy to see me. He never gets sad or feels lonely. I have a lot to learn from Bob. But sometimes I think I can learn a lot from my cat, Mango too. She doesn't have a party when I come home. Sometimes she's not at home at all, and when she arrives you don't even hear her. She is so cool and independent.

Should I be cool like Mango or happy like Bob? Or should I just be me, Emily28. But who am I now? Oh dear! It's all so confusing.

I don't tell my mum and dad about school because how can they understand? And they have enough problems with their new jobs, at their new schools. They are both teachers, you see. I don't want them to think that I'm no good and that nobody likes me.

I like it best when dad and I go fishing. We go to the lake near my school. It sounds boring, but it isn't. I like throwing little stones in the water. And then I watch the water move and make circles.

Plop!

I love the sound it makes. Dad says it disturbs the fish.

'Take it easy now' he says. 'The fish don't like that.'

But I think that dad likes watching the circles too. Dad knows that I'm not happy in my new town. When I sit there looking at the water, he looks at me and he asks,

'What is it?'

'Nothing' I reply. 'It's nothing.'

But he knows that something is wrong. There is something he wants to tell me. And sometimes he starts to speak, but then stops.

I tell my secret to the fish. They know about me, and they know about the bullies. I only tell you and them and Isabella because you are the only ones who won't tell anyone else.

12

Today is a good day because I'm writing to you. And now that we know each other a little I will tell you my real name.

It's Emma!

It's our secret now and not just mine. And I have another reason to be happy. Today is strawberry day. And what is strawberry day? Well, I will tell you.

In my new town there is a big jam factory. It makes the jam that you see in the supermarkets. It's really famous. Every day the factory makes a different kind of jam. On Monday they make strawberry jam.

And when they do this the whole town smells like strawberries.

Mmmmmm!

Delicious!

How can I be unhappy in a town that smells like strawberries?

It's the best thing about Monday and it's the first thing I notice when I open the door and leave my house to catch the bus to school.

I hope things will get better. I know they will. And soon Isabella will come to visit me.

Then the whole weekend will feel like a strawberry day!

Chapter Two: Who Is Egghead?

Tuesday February 7th, 2017

Today started well. I went to the lake before going to school. Everything is so quiet and peaceful there. It's my secret place.

I throw a stone into the water and hear the sound.

Plop!

And I watch the circles go round and round and round. And then I hear something. I hear a voice.

So late, so late!

I don't know where the voice comes from. Is it the sound of the water, or an animal, or is it the wind? I look around but I can't see anyone. What did the voice say? It said, 'so late, so late.' I look at my mobile phone and see that it's 9.05. The voice is right. I AM so late! I get up quickly and start running.

Run Emma Run! I say to myself. I want to get to school, but at the same time I don't want to get to school. The bullies are there! But I run.
Soon I'm in front of the school and soon I'm inside. I run down the corridor, and then I'm in front of the classroom door.

'Are you ready, Emma?' I say to myself. I'm not ready, but I push the door open very slowly and go inside. I don't want anyone to notice me. I just want to go to my seat and sit down quietly. But everyone, and I mean everyone turns their head to look at me.

The first thing I hear is Amy laughing.

'Farm Girl is here', says Chloe.

'She's late. But she can't help it. She can't tell the time,' says Amy.

'Be quiet' shouts Miss Smart, our teacher.

That's the way my morning starts. And it doesn't get any better.

During History, Miss Smart starts talking about the Roman Empire, but it's difficult to concentrate. That sound at the lake. What was it?

Emma!

There it is again, saying my name. It's a kind voice. Soft and kind. But where is it coming from? And then I understand. The voice is coming, from . . .
INSIDE MY HEAD!

'Emma! Emma!'

I hear my name again. But this time the sound is harder. It's an angry sound. This time the sound isn't inside my head. It's Miss Smart, outside my head, saying, 'Emma!'

'Sorry, Miss Smart' I say.
'You will be sorry,' says Miss Smart. 'First, you're late, then you're looking out of the window. What's the matter?'
'I don't know Miss. It's a voice, 'I said.
'Voice? What voice?'
'I'm not sure,' I said. 'It's not important'.
Now the whole class starts laughing.
'She's crazy,' says Amy.
Maybe Amy was right. Maybe I am crazy. But I wasn't frightened! The voice was friendly. It's inside me and it's helping me. I know that.
Before lunch we have Biology and after the lesson, I always help my teacher to clean up. I like looking at all the animals in the lab and when I do this I forget about Amy and Chloe. And Miss Percy, my biology teacher is so nice. It's good to spend time with her. I think I would like to do a job with animals when I'm older, or even to be a teacher of Biology or Art.

When I finish helping the teacher, I go to lunch. Amy and Chloe are waiting for me.
'Oh look, a creature from the lab,' shouts Chloe. 'We have to take it back to Miss Percy!'

I sit on my own at a table to eat lunch. It's chicken, peas, carrots, and potatoes.

'Don't give Farm Girl too many carrots,' says Amy.
I try to ignore her.

I close my eyes and imagine that I'm inside a bubble that protects me. In this bubble no one can make me feel bad.

I'm not hungry but I start to eat some potato. Then I hear the voice again,

Be careful! It's hot!

I touch the potato with my finger and yes, it's true. It is hot. I send a silent thank you to the voice, the voice that is here with me in my bubble. My new friend.

When the school bell rings, at the end of the day, it's a good sound to hear. I go home. I just want to go home. I want to get away from Chloe and Amy and all the others. But it's difficult to get away because the bullying doesn't stop when I get home.
It follows me into the house. I close the door, but I'm not safe. The bullies follow me in. They are here, with me, on my mobile phone.

I sit on my bed, and I look at my phone and start this little conversation with myself.
'Shall I look? Shall I look at WhatsApp?'
'No, I won't. There won't be anything good in there.'
But Isabella might be there. So maybe I should.'
'Will I, won't I?'
These are the games I play with myself every single day.
I want to look at the phone, but I don't want to look at it. It's like there is a kind of fight inside me. Shall I look or not? I always look in the end and lose.
I look. And, surprise, surprise! Chloe and Amy are there, saying horrible things about me on our class WhatsApp group.

Then I look at the laughing emojis. 1, 2, 3 faces laughing. Just laughing at me.

Why are Olivia, Abigail and Lucas sending these emojis? They don't say anything bad to me at school.

But then I think of that moment when Miss Smart was angry with me.

I remember their faces, laughing in class. They don't say anything bad to me, but they are just like Chloe and Amy. Maybe they are worse.

There are some in the class that don't laugh and don't say anything. They don't write on the WhatsApp group, and they don't send laughing emojis. Can they be my friends?

Isabella says that I should leave the WhatsApp group, but won't that make things worse?
No, it's me that has to change. I'm the one who is doing something wrong. I'm the new one. I just have to find a way to be the Emma I was in Norwich. To be a person that people like.

I'll try to find a way to stop these kinds of messages. I know I'll find a way. I just need a little bit more time.

I sit by my window and look out at the sea. In the distance I can see a lighthouse. It makes me feel better to look at it.

Should I delete the messages? But deleting them doesn't help me to forget them. I can't really delete them. They are there forever in my head.

And even if I delete the words, other people can read them. It's like having a tattoo that I can't wash away. That's why I try not to look at my mobile phone too much. But it's like I can't resist looking at it to check if there is something about me.
My mobile phone.
I love it and I hate it.
I hate it and I love it.
I can't live without it but it's difficult to live with it.
I want it but I don't want it.
It brings me sadness, but it also brings me happiness.

I can use it to speak to Isabella but at the same time, just as night follows day it also brings me those words, those horrible, cold unfriendly words.

'Egghead!'

It's the voice again. What is it saying this time?
Egghead?
Who is Egghead?

'Speak to Egghead!'

Chapter 3: The Lighthouse

Sunday March 5th, 2017

Isabella was here this weekend. We had an amazing time. I didn't think of Chloe and Amy, not even for one second. We went to the funfair, and we tried the rollercoaster. When you go up it's exciting because you know that soon you will have to go down, really fast. But I wasn't frightened. It was just me and Isabella and nobody else could touch us.

After the funfair, we walked along the beach and tried to take some cool selfies of each other with the lighthouse in the background. Isabella wants to post some of them and that's okay. In the online world I'm Emily28 and not Emma.

I didn't go swimming because the sea was very cold, but I love being by the sea. Isabella and I put our feet in the sea for a little while,

Brrrrrrrrrrrrr!!!

I love the sea because it feels like forever. In the water you can forget who you are. Everyone says that I'm very good at swimming, 'You swim like a fish,' they say.

I smile to myself and say thank you. But I don't think that I'm good. It's nothing special. It's the water that does everything. The water carries me, and it does all the hard work.

I like the sea because it changes all the time. Sometimes it's green and at other times it's blue. It can be angry or calm or sad and sometimes it seems like it wants to play with you.

Before bed I finish my drawing. Tomorrow, I will show it to my art teacher, Mr. Scott. Drawing helps me to forget all of my problems.

How can I explain it? It's like, when I draw, I make a little world of my own that feels safe. I can control it, I can feel it. Sometimes I want to jump inside it. It feels so good when I make a picture from nothing. It's like a new world that I create by myself and for myself.

After drawing I look out at the sea from my window. In the evening it's really special, and the colours are beautiful. I see the lighthouse in the distance. I feel calm watching the lighthouse send its light out into the night. The light brings the sea alive, and it keeps the ships at night safe so that they can find their way home.

Sometimes I feel like a ship that is lost at sea. And I really want the light from the lighthouse to come to

me. I need someone or something to help me find my way home.
But the light never comes.
It never will.

'Oh, it will come, and it will come soon.' says the voice.

Chapter 4: Egghead The Movie

Monday March 6th, 2017

I leave the house and walk to the bus stop. It's Monday again and everything smells of strawberries. I just had a fantastic weekend with Isabella. And I feel better about everything.

On the bus I think about Mango and Bob. Cats and dogs aren't normally friends, but Mango and Bob are. If they can be friends, why can't I be friends with my new classmates? I hope so, one day. I want that day to come. I want to make new friends so badly. But that day will not be today.

'There's nothing to worry about,' says the voice.

When I hear the voice again, I decide to give it a name. I close my eyes and think. And then I open them again.

SAFFY! Your name is Saffy. Thank you, Saffy I say, smiling. I get off the bus, still smiling.

'Emma, careful!' says Saffy.

I turn around but before I see it, I feel it. A push, then another push. I almost fall down. I can see who it is now. It's Amy and Chloe.
Then there is another push and suddenly I'm on the

ground. Everything goes dark for a minute.

Then I feel a hand pull me up.
'Where am I? What's happening?' I say to myself.
When I open my eyes I see Nathan, one of the bigger boys at school.
'Are you okay?' he asks.
Amy and Chloe aren't there anymore. Maybe seeing Nathan frightened them.

'Yes,' I say. 'Yes, . . .I'm, … Yes, . . . I'm, I'm okay thank you,'

But I wasn't okay. I decide to cross the road and take the bus home.
'No way am I going to school, today' I say to myself.
'I'm going home.'

But when I get home there is a surprise. I don't have my keys.

'They probably fell out of my pocket', I say to myself.
I knock on the door and shout,
'Mum! Mum! Mum!'
Mum opens the door and when I see her, I cannot control myself anymore. I start crying.
'What is it?' asks mum.
'They pushed me, pushed me like I was nothing. Like I was no one. A piece of trash!
They don't care if I live or die!'

'Who are they?' asks mum.

'You have never been bullied! You don't know what it's like' I add.

'You won't understand. You can't understand, so don't even try,' I shout.

And then I run to the bathroom and lock myself inside.

I stay in the bathroom for a long time because I hear mum near the door. I decide to take a shower. I want to wash off all the bad words and all the bad things. I want to wash them all away.

After the shower, when I'm sure that mum's not there I open the door and run down the hallway into my bedroom and close the door and the curtains.

When I'm on my bed I realise something,

'Oh no, my phone! It's not in my pocket! It's at the bus stop with my keys where Chloe and Amy pushed me!'

'Well, that's a good thing,' I say to myself. 'The phone just makes me sad.'

But I don't really believe that. It's not a good thing, and I start missing my phone.

Then I fall asleep. I dream about being outside a shop with big glass windows. Inside the shop I can see my mobile phone on the floor.

Chloe and Amy are inside the shop. They pick up the phone and start looking at it and writing things and I can't stop them. I bang on the window. I can't get in. Bang! Bang! Bang!

I wake up. The banging is my mum knocking at the door. I don't answer. And then I hear a noise. Something appears under the door.

A tiny thing in the darkness.

Was it food? Something to eat? But I wasn't hungry. I look closely and realise it's something else. It's not food. It's small and plastic. It's a USB drive!
Was it mum who put it there? Yes, who else can it be? Dad is at work and doesn't get home for another two hours, and Mango and Bob don't even know what a pen drive is. It was mum.
But why did she put it there?
I pick up the USB drive and turn on the computer. Then I put the pen drive in and wait to see what's inside.
There was one folder, and, on the folder, I see these words.

FOR ANDREW

I click on the folder, and inside I see a video. It's very old, made with an old film camera and then made into an MP4.
The image isn't clear.
There was a little boy talking in front of lots of other children.
In a school? It looks like a school assembly. I listen to the boy.

"My teacher asked our class to write about an important person in our lives. Well, there are many important people in my life, my mum, my dad, my uncle Terry, and auntie Kathie, but there is another person who is really special to me, and I want to tell you about him. His name is Tom. He helped me to understand that I should listen to people who know me and love me, and not listen to the people who call me Egghead and bully me. These people who bully me know nothing about me, so what they say is not important. Tom lives in our town. He is my friend, and he is a hero, a local hero. Do you know what he did for our town? He …."

It's only a short video, but at this point I stop listening for a moment. I need to think, to understand.
Who is Tom? And who is the boy who is speaking?
I watch the video until the end and then I watch it again and again and again, trying to understand.

And then I realise.

Then I hear another knock at the door. The door opens …
'Hello Cherub,'.
I look up. It's him! It's Egghead. The little boy in the video. But now he is a man, smiling at me.
Now he is . . .

MY DAD!

'I've got something to tell you,' said my dad.
'Me too,' I said.

That USB drive! Wow!!!
The person who made this film such a long time ago didn't know how important it was. The quality of the movie was bad. It was difficult to see the details. The colours were strange. It was a home movie made a long time ago on an old movie camera. But seeing it changed everything for me. For me to see dad there like that, a young boy who looked like me and had the same problem as me, made me feel different.

Chapter Five: Egghead, Farm Girl, Andrew & Saffy

Monday, March 6th, 2017

I look at dad, and he looks at me.
We don't speak for a little while.

We sit there for a minute or so. And then he pulls something out of his pocket.
'A boy came to our house and gave me this,' he said.
It was my mobile phone.
'Nathan found it!' I thought.

And then dad talks … and starts to answer the questions he can see on my face.

'Yes, that is me, in the video, when I was little. I was bullied every day at school, and it was difficult for me. Every day for me was a nightmare and everybody called me, Egghead.'

'Why didn't you say anything about it?' I ask.

'I'm sorry that I didn't tell you. I never talk to anyone about those times. When I left school, the bullying stopped. It was the end of a long story, the end of a long chapter of my life. I didn't want to think about it anymore. I wanted to stop being Egghead. But Egghead is always there,' he says pointing at his head. 'And Andrew is there too.'

'Who is Andrew?' I ask.

'When I was at school, there were two things that helped me to feel strong. One was a friend called Andrew. I talked to him every day and he talked to me. He was always there for me. He was a special friend. He helped me to believe in myself. But he was not like any other friend. He was different because .... he didn't exist!'

'What do you mean?' I ask.

He was an imaginary friend. He was a voice.

'Inside your head?'

'Yes, Emma. Yes!'

'I have a voice like that too,' I say. 'I call the voice, Saffy.'

'Saffy, Andrew. The name is not important. It's the voice that guides you. The voice you must listen to above all others. It's the voice that tells you one important thing.'
'What?'
'That you are okay. That you are perfect just as you are. Saffy is that part of you that no one can touch.

Saffy is for you and you alone.'

I thought about Saffy, and it's true. Saffy is that voice that tells me this. Saffy is for me. And in the quiet moments I can hear her voice. And it makes me feel better.
'And what's the second thing?' I ask.

'What do you mean?'

'You said there were two things that helped you at school.'

'Oh, the second thing was reading. I read stories like Black Beauty, The Railway Children, and Oliver Twist, every evening. I jumped inside those stories. It was a place I went to where nobody said bad things to me or called me names. I was a part of those stories. And it was the only time that I forgot about being Egghead and became Michael again.'

'But then every evening, I had to shut the book and become Egghead and I didn't want to be him. I believed that I was no good, a failure, a nobody. I believed what the boys and girls at school said about me.'

'How can I explain it?' continued dad. 'You know when you go to the cinema and watch a good movie.'
'Yes,' I said.

'Well, when you watch the film, you forget about yourself.'

'Yes, that's true. If I watch a good film, I stop thinking about my problems,' I said.

'And then the lights come on. On the screen you see the words, THE END. And you have to leave the cinema and go back to your life. That is what it was like for me every time I closed my book.'

'You still read a lot now', I said.

'Yes, because when you read, you are never alone.'

'It's the same for me when I draw. I forget about me and my problems. Drawing helps me.'

'I know,' says dad. 'There are many things we have in common.'

And I believed for the first time, that dad really did know. I believed that he did understand. And I knew that I wasn't alone. But I had another question.

'But why did they call you Egghead?'
'Do you know, after all these years, I still don't really know. I had lots of hair. I still have lots of hair. My head was quite big with all the hair. But it's not important. It's just silly. What do they call you?'

'Farm Girl,' I said.

And when I said it for some reason dad, and I started laughing.

How stupid it all was. When Farm Girl and Egghead stopped laughing, I had one more question for dad.

'In the film you talk about Tom. Who was Tom?'

'He was a friend. I saw him as an old man because he was much older than me. He listened to me, and he taught me something very important.'

'What was it?'

'These people who bully you, what are their names?'

'Chloe and Amy. They are the ones who bully me the most.'
'Well, Chloe and Amy do not know you. If they don't know you, what they think of you is not important.'
'I see. It's what you said in the video, in front of the school'.

'Yes,' that's right. What do Chloe and Amy know about you? I mean really know.'

'They know that I come from Norwich.'

'And, what else?'

'Well, they know …', I said.
But I stopped speaking because I couldn't finish my sentence. Dad was right. They know nothing about me.
They don't know that I like drawing. They have no idea that I love rollercoasters and that I like to put my feet in the sea. They don't know that my favourite food is lasagne. They don't know that I have a friend called Isabella, that I cry when I see a sad movie, that my favourite colour is blue. They don't know that I like the smell of strawberry jam. They don't know that I wake up every single day hoping that this will be the day that I finally find a friend.
I put my hair in front of my eyes like a curtain. At this moment, I don't want dad to see my eyes.
Because I am crying behind a curtain of hair.
Dad hugs me and waits for the crying to stop. I needed that hug. And when I stop crying, he starts to speak.

'The people who called me names, all those years ago didn't want to know me. They called me Egghead. To them I was just Egghead. They never wanted to know me. When I left that school, I never saw any of them again. I didn't want to see them again. If I see them on the street, it will be like seeing a person I do not know, a stranger. Don't give away what is precious about you, don't lose the sense of who you are and what is special about you to people who don't know anything about you. Think about it. These are people who don't know who Emma is. They only know that you come from Norwich, and what are they saying about Norwich?'

'That people there are all slow and stupid,' I said.

'Which means that they don't know Norwich either, having never spent even one minute there. What they say is not important,' said dad.
I could understand what dad was saying. It made sense. But why was it important for them to like me? Why did I need it so much?

Now I had another question for dad.
'Why didn't you talk about being bullied after you left school?' I asked.
And dad tried to explain,
'I just wanted to forget about this period of my life. I didn't want to be Egghead anymore, even in my memories. And so, I forgot about it and went to a different school. Then to university. Then I met your mum and we got married and then you arrived. And here we are again, life has this habit of making

circles, like the ones you make at the lake.'
'And now I see Egghead again,' said dad, smiling as he turned towards the frozen image on the computer screen.

When dad left my bedroom, I looked at the image on the screen, frozen in time. At the time dad made that video he believed that he was always going to be Egghead. He couldn't see a future where he wasn't Egghead. He didn't believe that he could be happy, get a good job, find a wife, and have children. But now he is smiling. He was able to forget about it, and not talk about it, and start a new life. That made me feel better. If dad could do this, then so could I.

'I won't always be Farm Girl,' I said to myself. 'But I can't live in the future. I can only live in the now. And right now, there are some problems. Their names are Amy and Chloe. What am I going to do about them?'

Chapter Six: Like a Fish

Tuesday, March 7th, 2017

When dad and I go fishing we always catch a fish. But we never take it home. We throw it back in the water.

I tell my secrets to the fish because they are like me. Every day I go home but I know that the next day I will be a fish that someone will catch, when I go to school.

But now, after watching dad's movie things seem a little different. I'm not alone. My dad understands me. And Saffy? How did she know about Egghead? I'm so happy that I have her. They don't know me. The others in my class don't know me. So how can what they say be important? I say this to myself while I work on my latest drawing.

Do you remember the special drawing I told you about, in January? Well, some time ago I showed it to my art teacher, Mr. Scott. I was a bit nervous about showing him.

'Very good Emma! Excellent! Can I keep it for a few days?' he said.

'Yes, of course, sir,' I replied .

I don't know why he wants to keep it. Maybe he wants to put it up on the classroom wall. But that was about two weeks ago and it's not on the wall. Maybe I should ask him to give it back.

Dad says that he is going to write a story about that

time, when he was a little boy. And he is going to call the story, 'Egghead'. I hope that lots of children read it. It will help them to understand.

It's the evening. The sky is dark, and I look out of the window at the lighthouse.
I pick up my phone and click on WhatsApp.
And then I leave the group.
I can do that because now I know. I know that I'm not the only fish in the sea.

Chapter 7: Egghead is Born

Tuesday March 7th, 2017

Speaking to Emma last night helped me to understand. I have to become that little boy again and write his story.

There are many Eggheads in the world today, even more than when I was that boy.

And it is more difficult for children now. When I was a young boy, I was safe when I got home. I could close my bedroom door, and no one could touch me. Now it's not like that.

It will be a true story. I will remember the details as I write.

Then, I can use this story to help children who need to know that they are not alone.

Chapter 8: Dots are Dancing!

Wednesday March 8th, 2017

It's strange how one click can cause such a reaction. I arrive at school and people who never say anything to me, start speaking.
'Why did you leave?'
'Amy is really angry'.
'Keep away from Chloe, she's mad at you.'
'I want to leave the group too. It's not a nice group. People only say bad things to each other.'
'Let's make a new group.'
'What are you going to say to Amy and Chloe?'
Just by clicking I seem to be the person of the moment. It's all so silly. I needed to leave the group and so I left. But it's not the end of the world, is it?'

'No, it isn't,' said Saffy.

Then I hear them. The other people who were speaking to me before are silent again as Chloe and Amy come into the classroom and start to speak.
'Oh, here she is.'
'Too good for our group, is she?'
'Well, don't come back, Farm Girl. We don't want you and we will block you if you try.'
'I'm not coming back,' I said. 'I, I …' but I don't have time to say anything else, at that moment Mr. Scott walks into the classroom and starts speaking.

'Why is he looking at me?' I ask myself. 'Does he know about me leaving the group?'

'Emma, stand up please.'

'Oh no!! Was it so bad to leave the group?' I say to myself. 'Is Mr Scott angry with me, about it? But why is he smiling?'

I stand up.

'I want to congratulate you, Emma! And I think the whole class should congratulate you.'

'Congratulate me? What's going on?' I ask myself.

'Listen!' says Saffy.

'Class. Did you know that Emma is an artist? She draws beautiful pictures.'
The teacher looked around the class. Nobody knows this of course.
Nobody has ever looked at any of my paintings.
Nobody knows that I love drawing. Nobody knows anything about me.

'Well, Emma showed me a picture she has drawn recently. And I liked it. I liked it so much that I sent it to the organisers of a competition for young artists in the UK and Emma is in the final.'

In the final!! Me??? Little me??? But I am no one. I am nothing. I am . . . in the final.

'Yes, you're in the final,' says Saffy.

'That means that someone likes what I do.
Someone likes my drawings. Little me!!! Did you hear that, Saffy? I cannot believe it.'

I forget all about the WhatsApp group, and Chloe and Amy and all the problems at school. It's thanks to my teacher. He believed in me and now look at what has happened.
Not bad for a simple farm girl, is it?
You cannot see the smile of an imaginary friend. But you can feel it.
And Saffy was smiling at me.

I don't remember anything else that happened on that day at school. I don't even remember how I got home. It felt like I was flying.
I kept replaying that moment in my head when the teacher said to me,

'Emma is in the final!'
It doesn't matter if my drawing wins or not. Just the fact that someone likes my drawing makes me feel like I can fly.

'You know what, Saffy?' I say that evening. 'I feel

like Dumbo the elephant. Have you ever seen that movie? Maybe invisible friends can't see movies. It's a Disney movie, quite an old one. Dumbo is an elephant with big ears who lives in the circus. Lots of other animals in the circus laugh at him and tell him he is no good. But he is friends with the birds.'
'Well, in the movie Dumbo wants to fly like his friends. The birds teach him that if he believes he can fly, he can.'
'And so, Dumbo flies around in the circus tent. I know how Dumbo feels. I feel light. Now I know that I can fly.'

I am sure the dots are dancing now in the WhatsApp group as everyone writes about me. But I don't care. I can fly!

And so, I fly inside my house to tell mum and dad the news. I won't tell you what they said, and how they reacted. I won't tell you about the hugs and the smiles. I am sure that you can imagine their joy.

I will close the door of my house just for a little while so that I can enjoy a little bit of time on my own with mum and dad. And I will speak to you later.

Goodnight for now.

Chapter 9: Unique Style!

Friday July 21st, 2017

Lots of things have happened since I last wrote here. I'm sorry! There was no time to write. I have done lots of drawings and so many things have happened.

Dad has been busy too. He finished his story. It only took him three months to write. He said it was easy because the story was already in his head. And Andrew was in his head too to help him write it. Soon he will have the book in his hands, and he wants to use it to tell children like me that they are never alone.I was the first person to read dad's story. He read every chapter to me, and I listened to every word. I hope that you read it too one day.

Saffy is with me now.

We are sitting with Isabella by the river in Norwich. It's summertime and I am back here with her in a place where I cannot smell the strawberries. I will do that again when I go back home. And yes, finally my new town feels a bit like home.

I know that everything will be fine. I have made some new friends, not many but enough.

Finally!

And we chat on WhatsApp. I don't need a WhatsApp group. I know who my real friends are without a group. They are the people who really want to know me.

What happened in the competition? I hear you say. Well, I will tell you.

I won!!!!

My drawing won first prize. I didn't believe it at first when Mr Scott told me. I have never won anything before. But the judges said that my drawing was the best. They gave the school five new computers and some software to help students with their artwork. I also won lots of cool art books and soon I'm going away for a week to an Art Workshop in Scotland.

There was a ceremony at the school. It was in the newspaper.

EMMA'S UNIQUE STYLE
WINS HER FIRST PLACE IN ART COMPETITION

That's what the newspaper said.

Unique Style!!! Wow!!!

Chloe and Amy leave me alone now. I think they know that their words can't touch me anymore. I don't need them to like me.

I have Bob and Mango, my mum and dad and Saffy. I have Isabella and my new friends. And I have my Art.

Would you like to see the drawing? The drawing that won first prize.
I'm sure you would. And if you are reading me, you know what this picture means.
Here it is.
Do you like it? Mango does.

And I hope you do too.

Sing Along!

Got Something To Tell You
(Paoloni/Lacey Freeman)

Every day I can see your face, in the rain
In the darkness

Take it easy now, Tell me why and how
Take it easy now, Tell me why and how

Every day I can see that place, in my pain
It's my business

Dots are Dancing 1, 2, 3
Are you reading me?

Got something to tell you
It's so late
See it in my fate
Being in the race

Got something to tell you
It's so late
See it in my fate
Being in the race

Take it easy now, Tell me why and how
Take it easy now, Tell me why and how

Every day I can see your face, in the rain
In the darkness

Dots are Dancing 1, 2, 3
Are you reading me?

Got something to tell you
It's so late
See it in my fate
Being in the race

Got something to tell you
It's so late
See it in my fate
Being in the race

Dots are Dancing 1, 2, 3
Dots are Dancing 1, 2, 3
Dots are Dancing 1, 2, 3
Are you reading me?

Got something to tell you
Got something to tell you

Take it easy now, Tell me why and how
Take it easy now, Tell me why and how

Take it easy now, Tell me why and how
Take it easy now, Tell me why and how

Beside You
(Paoloni/Lacey Freeman)

I saw the smile on your face.
By your side, and at my place.
Under the guidance of your eyes.
Making the world the greatest prize.

Nothing can change you all these years.
Taking me farther from my fears.
Nothing can be the same, without you.
Oh! Beside you.

We played for hours on the street.
Living the dreams, we chanced to meet.
Under the garden of your eyes.
Making the world a great surprise.

Nothing can change you all these years.
Taking me farther from my fears
Nothing can be the same, without you.
Oh!
Nothing can change you all these years.
Giving me comfort from my fears

Nothing can be the same, without you.
Oh!
Beside you.

Feeling nothing can be changed.
Feeling nothing can be changed.

Doo doo doo doo doo doo doo.

Oh!

Nothing can change.
Nothing can change.
Nothing can change.
We are beside you.
Nothing can change.
Nothing can change.
Nothing can change you know without you.
Oh! Beside you.

I saw the smile on your face.
By your side, and at my place.
Under the guidance of your eyes.
Making the world the greatest prize.

About the Author

The Writer
Hello! My name is Michael Lacey Freeman, and I am the writer of this story. Thank you for reading. Many years ago, I was bullied, both mentally and physically. Every day, when I went to school, someone tried to make me feel that I was no good, a freak, a failure. I believed what the bullies said about me.

But now I understand that the experience made me stronger. I wanted to write a story with a simple message. Do not let the bullies take away what is precious about you. They have no idea who you are. Bullies are not interested in knowing you, so what they think is not important. They do not know you.

The Stories
I have written many stories over the last ten years. I have also written adaptations of classic stories like Anne of Green Gables, Black Beauty, The Railway Children and Mill on the Floss. Some people take photos, other people dance, or enjoy making things.

Everyone has something that makes them feel better when they have a problem. I love writing stories because it makes me happy.

Egghead The Movie

When I travel around schools and meet readers all over the world, I answer many questions about my stories, about bullying in general. I wrote Egghead the Movie to answer some of these questions. Sadly, bullying is a problem everywhere and in every country. With this story I want to tell readers that bullying is not forever. I am happy now, and even if you are bullied you will be happy one day too.

An Invitation to Listen

Cyberbullying makes life even harder for children who are bullied now. Bullies ignore you. Ignorance is nothing more than a decision to ignore. When you hear someone's story you do not want to bully them because you know them. So, listen to the stories of others. If you see someone who is alone and needs help, send them a smiley icon, say hello, or ask how they are. And listen to their stories. You can make a difference.

Michael accepting the ERF Language Learner Literature Award, Tokyo 2017

About the Illustrators

Craig Bulloch

Hello! I'm Craig, and I worked with Bethany and Michael to make this story. I really enjoyed working with Bethany on the drawings. It's so cool to think that people all over the world will see our drawings. I like travelling and I would like to learn about and experience the many different cultures around the world. I love illustration and that is why I studied this subject at university. It is not just a hobby, and not just a job. It is a passion! Another great passion of mine is Graphic Design. When working with Bethany on the illustrations for Egghead the Movie it was great to use the things I have learnt at college and university. I would like to thank two teachers who helped me when I was a student at Harlow college. Thanks to them I learnt so many things.

I hope you like what we have done!

You can find my work on Instagram and Facebook!

Instagram: ryukicomics
Facebook: Ryuki Comics

Bethany Lacey-Freeman

Hi! I'm Bethany, and I am the artist behind most of the illustrations in this book! This book has been a real passion project for me, and I have put all my love and attention into each of these illustrations. I was born in England in 1995, and at the age of 5, my family and I moved to Florida, USA! My childhood and teen years in the states were super fun and I can't wait to go back one day and see all my old friends! I have always been passionate about art, and when my family and I returned back to England in 2014, I studied Graphic Design at Colchester Institute, and then Illustration at Norwich University of the Arts, where I got my bachelor's degree!

Working with Craig to Illustrate and design this book has been great fun, and I can't wait to work with him and Michael more in the future to bring you all more great stories!

You can find my work on Instagram and Facebook!

Instagram: bethlf_illustrates
Facebook: Bethany
Lacey-Freeman Illustration

65

About the Music

Our Music

Hi there! We are two people who make music. Our names are Michael Lacey Freeman and Lorenzo Paoloni. The music we make is connected to stories like the one you are reading now. We have made lots of songs and we hope that you listen to more of them when you finish reading this story. At the back of the book, you will see some links that will help you to find some more of our music.

Got Something to Tell You

The theme tune to Egghead the Movie is the song, 'Got Something to Tell You'. If you read carefully almost all the words in the song are in the story. The song was written in 2017 but we didn't finish it until 2023. The lyrics were written especially for this story. We hope you like it. There are another two songs called, 'Beside You,' and 'I'm Afraid' which are also connected to the story. Very soon we are going to make an album of our songs.

Lorenzo Paoloni

Hi! My name is Lorenzo and I work with Michael in making music for the stories he writes. I am a musician, and I can play many different instruments. I love all kinds of music but for me the greatest band of all time will always be The Beatles.

Across The Sky

The lyrics to our songs are very important. They help to tell the story. Sometimes people will listen to the song first and then read the story. Or they will read the story and then listen to the song.

Our most famous songs are 'Crying' and 'Across the Sky'. 'Crying' is a story about bullying. 'Across the Sky' is a message of hope. Many children sang 'Across the Sky' during the pandemic. The message of the song is, We Can Do It!

Test your Memory

1 What is Emma's name on Instagram and why did she choose it?

2 What jobs do Emma's mum and dad have?

3 What day is strawberry day?

4 What are the first words that Saffy says to Emma?

5 Name three of Emma's teachers.

6 What are the names of the two bullies?

7 Where does Emma go with Isabella at the weekend?

8 Where did the bullies push Emma?

9 What did Emma leave on the ground after being pushed?

10 What name does Emma's dad give her?

11 Who was Tom?

12 What does 'dots are dancing' refer to?

13 What Disney character does Emma compare herself to?

14 What prizes did Emma win in the art competition?

15 How many times does water play a part in the story?

16 Who said this? Match the words to the character.

Amy. Emma. Emma's dad. Mr. Scott. Nathan. Saffy

A 'I've got something to tell you'. . . . .

B 'So late! So late!' . . . .

C 'Who is Egghead?' . . . .

D 'Did you hear that Emma is an artist?' . . . .

E 'Are you okay?' . . . .

F 'Don't give farm girl any carrots.' . . . .

A Week of Jam

Monday

Tuesday

Wednesday

Thursday

Friday

Saturday
& Sunday

BONUS STORY
Mr. Smart

By Michael Lacey Freeman

When I found out that all children had to go to school, I tried very hard to imagine what it would be like for me. I was only four years old and was very curious.

What was in that place? And why did I have to go there?
I would close my eyes and imagine sitting at a desk in front of an enormous clock, waiting for the bell to ring to go home.
That is what I thought that school was like.

When I finally started going to school, I didn't like it. I was horrified by the idea that I had to go there every day for at least eleven years. Eleven years for a five-year-old is more than two lifetimes.

I was the kind of boy that sat in the corner, trying very hard not to be noticed. My body was in the classroom, but not my mind. My mind was outside the four walls of the class. I soon found out that I didn't sit with a big clock in front of me, but there was indeed a lot of waiting. School was somewhere I didn't want to be, and I had to wait a long time to not be there.

Being noticed at school was dangerous for me. No, it was best to be ignored and unnoticed. It was safer. I just wanted to do my exercises and then slip outside of school and get back to my bedroom where I could read stories and listen to music.

School was rarely enjoyable for me simply because it was too full of other people. I lived in an imaginary world of my own with imaginary friends. When I went home, I went home to the company of Me, Myself and I.

Little by little of course I made some friends, but I was only close to two of them. I had a friend called David and we would run around the playground together and talk about what was on the TV, and what stories we liked best. We read every book in the school library. The library was small and our appetite for stories was big.

I also had an imaginary friend called Andrew. He was my best friend because he lived inside my head and was only there for me. He would inspire and whisper encouragement from within and I felt stronger and comforted by this voice.

I needed Andrew for many years. He helped me to deal with the constant mental and physical bullying that accompanied me through my school life.

I remember one moment, when I walked into the school changing room to get ready for my swimming lesson. As soon as they saw me, the class before me who were changing back into their school uniforms started to sing a song, they had made up about me.

I still remember that song and how much it hurt to think that they went to all that effort just to do something to make me feel smaller.

But on that day, guided by Andrew, I lifted up my hands and moved them around, pretending to be the conductor of an orchestra, an orchestra of people who despised me, even if they didn't know anything about me at all.

A choir of ignorance.

Bullying is all about ignorance. It is a decision to ignore the victim and to be uninterested in his or her story. The bullies didn't want to know anything about me. They didn't know that I loved reading. They had no idea that I played football by myself and went to the park every morning with my dog who was called, Ben. They didn't know that I had an imaginary friend called Andrew and that I spent every day of my life waking up and hoping and praying that this would be the day that I would finally start to feel that I belonged.

Being a conductor in that moment was part of a strategy I had. I needed to hide, behind humour, or behind a desk, finding the corner of every room I sat in, looking anxiously towards the doors and the windows of the room, my escape routes. And needed to look out of those windows because I wanted with every bone in my body to be outside the classroom.

Well, for many years now I have been outside that classroom. When I left school, I said goodbye to Andrew, but sometimes he returns when I need him. I also said goodbye to David, but sometimes we meet and talk about those old times.

Now I don't have to be inside that classroom, looking out of the window. I don't have to be on the inside looking out. I can be on the outside, looking in. I am a grown man, and my school days are a distant memory. And now, when I look inside closely, I can even see some good things, and good people. People who shaped me and guided me and helped me to be happy.

Those people are called, teachers.

There was Mrs. Hewitt who gave me a big pile of books to read when she found out that I loved reading stories. I loved those stories. At first, I read them for her, to please her. But soon I was reading them for myself.

When I wrote my first story, I put the book under my arm and went back to my hometown in London. I found a street and looked for a house. When I found the house, I opened the gate and went inside. I knocked on the door and the door opened. A face appeared. It was Mrs. Hewitt. It was over thirty years later, but it was her. And she remembered me.

I suddenly felt like I was 13 years old again and not 50. I handed her the book and said,

'Thank you'.

There was Mr. Tyll who taught me to draw. I always wanted to draw enormous landscapes so that I could be like a little dot in a field or a tiny speck on a boat in the ocean. Even in my drawings I was hardly noticeable. Not really there.

Once Mr. Tyll took me aside after class and we went for a walk. He told me that everything was going to be okay. I didn't believe him. I thought that he was just being nice. But he was right.

Thank you Mr. Tyll! I never had the opportunity to thank you in person. You left this world before I had the chance. But

Thank you!

And then there was Mr. Smart.

Mr. Smart told us stories. Stories about The Russian Revolution, The Cultural Revolution, The Normans, The Vikings, The Romans, the Renaissance.

So many stories

He was my history teacher and his words transported me to other times and other places. I remember his stories from 1917, the year of the Russian Revolution. On that day during the lesson, I cut my finger by accident. I don't remember how. And some blood fell on my exercise book. I looked at the blood and imagined that it was blood from the revolution.

The pages turned in my head. The years went by. My love for those stories remained thanks to my history teacher, Mr. Smart.

My favourite stories were the ones about Italy. In my little head I decided that one day I was going to live there. I didn't know how I was going to do it. But I knew that I would. I just had to. Mr. Smart took me there so many times that it was a place that was destined to stay inside my head and my heart forever.

I was still that quiet boy in the corner who hoped not to be noticed. But my mind and not just my body was in that classroom when Mr. Smart walked in.

One day he walked into class and started giving us back our homework. He would chat to every student, telling them what was good about the work and how they could do a little bit better. He always did that. And then he came to me and placed my work on the desk. I looked down and saw a big fat A, scrawled on the paper. I looked up and saw him smiling at me.

'Yours is the best, Freeman! Keep it that way!'

They were nine words that changed my life.

Mr. Smart I have tried to keep it that way. All of my life. And I will keep on trying. I never said good-bye to you, but I also never said goodbye to your stories. I kept on studying History and doing my best. I went on to college and got the top mark in History. I was told that it was the top mark in the whole county and that it was good enough to get into Oxford University. But I wasn't ready to believe that I could manage such a thing. I was still that little speck in the ocean. I studied History at another university and did well.

And then, one day I was at Heathrow Airport in London. I was 26 years old and was saying goodbye to a friend who was going to New York. After saying goodbye, I turned to leave for home. Home was a city called Norwich where I had a good job and a nice house. Things were going well for me.

I looked up and saw a newspaper stand in front of me. I cast my eyes down at newspapers displayed there from all over the world.

El Pais, Le Monde, Bild, The New York Times

But my eyes stopped at an Italian newspaper.

'Il Corriere della Sera'

And then I heard a voice. A familiar voice.
No, it wasn't Mr. Smart.

It was Andrew. And he said,

'It's time!'

I went home and told my boss that very day that I was leaving. Then I told my landlord. Then I did the most difficult thing of all, one of the most difficult things I have ever had to do. I told my mother.

I still thank my mother to this day for not crying when I told her that I was leaving the UK for Italy. My father told me that she saved her tears for later, when I wasn't there.

One month later I was in that airport again. Not to say goodbye to a friend. But to move to Italy. I have lived in this beautiful country ever since.

It is a place I am proud to call my home.

Teachers are the conductors of an orchestra, and every student plays a different instrument in that orchestra.

Teachers help us to make the music in our heads that will be the soundtrack to our lives.

Thank you, Mr. Smart, Mr. Tyl and Mrs. Hewitt for helping to make the music so beautiful!

Useful Links

Michael's Website - search:
www.michaellaceyfreeman.com
on internet browser, or scan the QR code below:

 On my web site you can find some comprehension and grammar activities for Egghead the Movie. There are also many other surprises including some short stories and songs. Audio file available.

'Across the Sky' Karaoke Version - search:
Across the Sky lyrics | Think Big theme song

 Thousands of people have listened to this song. Sing along to this karaoke version of Across the Sky which we made in 2020.

Egghead's YouTube Channel - search on YouTube:
Lorenzo Paoloni & Michael Lacey Freeman

Here you can find the songs from the story: 'Got Something to Tell You', 'Beside You', and 'I'm Afraid'.

Egghead's Facebook page - search: *Michael LF*
on Facebook, or scan the QR code below

 On this page you can post the drawings you do or stories you write and share them with other readers.

Test Your Memory - Answers:

1. Emily28 – She lived in 28a Cardiff Road when Norwich was her home
2. They are teachers
3. Monday
4. So late, So late
5. Miss Smart, Mr. Scott, Miss Percy
6. Amy and Chloe
7. To the funfair and then to the beach
8. At the bus stop
9. Her keys and her mobile phone
10. Cherub
11. Tom was Michael's friend, and he talked about him at the school assembly
12. When someone is writing to you online three dots move up and down
13. Dumbo
14. Five new computers, software, art books, and an art workshop in Scotland for one week
15. Water plays a major role in the story. Emma goes to the lake, she loves the sea, and she tries to wash away the pain when she has a shower. Water is a calming place for her

16A. Emma's dad
16B. Saffy
16C. Emma
16D. Mr. Scott
16E. Nathan
16F. Amy